Ultra-Solutions

Ultra-Solutions

W. W. NORTON & COMPANY

New York   London

or
How to Fail
Most
Successfully

PAUL WATZLAWICK

Published simultaneously in Canada by Penguin Books
Canada Ltd., 2801 John Street, Markham, Ontario L3R 1B4.
Printed in the United States of America.

The text of this book is composed in Aster, with display type
set in Aster. Composition and manufacturing by The Haddon
Craftsmen, Inc.
Book design by Jacques Chazaud.

First Edition

Library of Congress Cataloging-in-Publication Data

Watzlawick, Paul.
   Ultra-solutions, or, How to be a success at failure.

   Translation of: Vom Schlechten des Guten.
   Bibliography: p.
   1. Happiness—Anecdotes, facetiae, satire, etc.
2. Problem-solving—Anecdotes, facetiae, satire, etc.
3. Double bind (Psychology)—Anecdotes, facetiae,
satire, etc.   4. Paradox—Anecdotes, facetiae, satire,
etc.   5. Psychology, Pathological—Anecdotes, facetiae,
satire, etc.   I. Title.   II. Title: Ultra-solutions.
III. Title: How to be a success at failure.
BF575.H27W3813   1988   158   87–24735

ISBN 978-0-393-33376-3

W.W. Norton & Company, Inc.
500 Fifth Avenue, New York, N. Y. 10110
W.W. Norton & Company Ltd.
37 Great Russell Street, London WC1B 3NU

1 2 3 4 5 6 7 8 9 0

Contents

CONTENTS

8

Author's Note

There exists a certain type of solution which does not have a name of its own in general parlance, but which may best be called an *ultra-solution*. Such a solution not only does away with the problem, but also with just about everything else, somewhat in the vein of the old medical joke—Operation successful, patient dead—with which we are all familiar. Thus, only the name suggested here is new, the hubris to which it refers has always been with us. Let me illustrate this with a famous example: the fate of Macbeth.

While many of Shakespeare's characters are dark and enigmatic, the role of the three witches in *Macbeth* is fairly straightforward. Their boss, Hecate, the sinister goddess of the underworld in Greek mythology, has instructed the witches to prepare Macbeth's downfall by leading him to believe that his future holds the fulfillment of his most ambitious desires—a prophecy that he is all the more willing to believe as it heightens his intoxication with the idea of ultimate power. In the attempt to reach that goal, Macbeth becomes easy prey to Hecate's machinations.

Why Hecate should devote all her energy and skill into orchestrating Macbeth's doom (and, as we shall see, that of many other people) is a question to which nobody seems to have the answer. *That* this is what Hecate wants and finally achieves, is obvious. *How* she manages to set up the preconditions for ultra-solutions is what this book wants to document; not only with regard to Macbeth, but also in a number of contemporary cases. For it may not be generally known that the subversive activities of the Hecate-team are by no means limited to Macbeth and the eleventh century, but are timeless —albeit with the important difference that the modern techniques now available to Hecate are a far cry from what they were nine centuries ago. But the common denominator, that is, the *principle* underlying all the strategies of Hecate clearly reveals itself in the case of Macbeth.

Author's Note

The prophecies of the witches have brought Macbeth to the point of no return, "I am in blood/stepp'd in so far that, should I wade no more,/returning were as tedious as go o'er." [III/4] But he still vacillates, "My strange and self-abuse/is the initiate fear, that wants hard use," [III/4] and is thus insufficiently prepared for his catastrophe. This inept handling of the case by her subordinates arouses Hecate's anger and makes it necessary for her to take charge personally:

> . . . How did you dare
> To trade and traffic with Macbeth
> In riddles and affairs of death;
> And I, the mistress of your charms,
> The closest contriver of all harms,
> Was never call'd to bear my part,
> Or show the glory of our art? [III/5]

And how does Hecate succeed in preventing Macbeth from reconsidering the whole business, from somehow trying to atone for the horrors already committed and trying to save what still can be saved? Please note, it is not by trying to convince him that he is on the right course, nor by encouraging him to commit the ultimate evil or by persuading him to trust implicitly his good fortune. These and any other luke-warm incitements one might think of are not part of her strategy. No, she instructs the witches to lull Macbeth into a sense of total security:

He shall spurn fate, scorn death, and bear
His hopes 'bove wisdom, grace and fear;
And you all know, security
Is mortals' chiefest enemy. [III/5]

And to make him trust his security beyond all reason, the witches are instructed to mention to Macbeth two circumstances that seem so unlikely that he can safely disregard them. The first:

Be bloody, bold, and resolute; laugh to scorn
The power of man, for none of woman born
Shall harm Macbeth. [IV/1]

Since this rules out just about every human being, Macbeth, need not even fear Macduff, his most dangerous enemy. The second:

Macbeth shall never vanquish'd be until
Great Birnam wood to high Dunsinane hill
Shall come against him. [IV/1]

Now he feels secure and ready to commit the decisive atrocities. The only trouble is that—thanks to a limited knowledge of obstetrics—Macbeth *is* slain by Macduff, who came into this world by Cesarean section, while the enemy army, camouflaged with leaves, advances like a giant forest, on his castle, Dunsinane.

As already pointed out, Macbeth is only *one,*

although perhaps the best-known, of Hecate's cases. Her activities stretch far back into Dionysian times, and up to our present day. I have uncovered evidence of much more recent cases to which Hecate has applied her ultra-solutions —or is in the process of doing so—in order to bring disaster into the world. Detailed investigations, extending over many years, now enable me to present concrete evidence of her specific tactics. Professional ethics of course forbid me to reveal my sources of information, and all identifying features, such as the names of persons or of places, have been altered. Furthermore, it must be borne in mind that Hecate no longer roams the dark of night in her ancient guise of three-armed specter, surrounded by packs of howling dogs, and casting spells and bewitching people. Rather, she lives in an elegant villa overlooking the blue Mediterranean, a retreat whose *surface* appearance seems as harmless as her sophisticated techniques, based on the latest technical achievements.

I want to start by reporting on a particular case and then return to this same case at the end of the book. Since the most appropriate cover name, *Everyman,* has already been used by the Austrian playwright Hugo von Hofmannsthal, I shall call the person I'm writing about simply "our man," in order to avoid plagiarism. And to prevent being considered sexist, let me say that "our man" means "our woman" too.

Ultra-Solutions

1

Security Is Mortals' Chiefest Enemy

Once upon a time there was a man who lived happily and in peace with himself and the world, until one day—perhaps out of senseless curiosity, perhaps out of sheer levity—he asked himself if life has its own rules. He was not referring to the obvious fact that every country in the world has its own customs and legal codes,—for instance, belching after a meal may be considered rude in one society and a compliment to the hostess in another or people should not scribble graffiti on walls if they cannot spell. No, these were not the issues; such rules invented by humans for humans were of little interest to him. What he suddenly wanted, needed, to know was whether life has its *own* regularities, quite independently of us.

If only he had never asked himself this accursed question, for it spelled the end of his happiness and contentment. It threw him into the same predicament as that experienced by the centipede when the cockroach innocently wanted to know how he managed to move his hundred legs with such elegance and ease. The centipede started thinking—and from that moment on he was unable to walk.

To put it less trivially: What happened to our man was similar to what Saint Peter experienced when he leaped from the boat and ran towards Christ—until it occurred to him that walking on water, as Jesus was doing, was utterly impossible. Whereupon Peter promptly sank into Lake Genesareth and almost drowned. (As is well known, sailors and fishermen usually cannot swim.)

Our man who asked about life was too sharp a thinker, and that was part of his problem. By his reasoning, the question of whether the world has an intrinsic order was tantamount to the question of its (and thus his own) security, and the answer to this question had to be either *yes* or *no*. If the answer was *no*, but here he hesitated. . . . A random world, a life without reliable order? How then had he managed to live happily until now, on what basis had he made his decisions? Would this not mean that the tranquil certainty about his place in the world and the serenely self-evident logic of his actions were really absurd and irrational?

With this, our man had eaten from the Tree of Knowledge, but the knowledge gained from this snack only further proved his ignorance. And instead of sinking into the waters of Lake Genesareth he plunged into an underground hovel similar to that from which Dostoevsky's anti-hero had directed his tirades against the world above:

> I swear, gentlemen, that to be too conscious is an illness—a real thoroughgoing illness. [. . .] You know, the direct, legitimate fruit of consciousness is inertia, that is, conscious sitting-with-the-hands-folded.

No, our man did not want to become like that famous writer of *The Letters from Underground.* A pessimist would probably have said that he had *not yet* taken that route. For he still hoped to discover that the world was based on logic and reason and predictability; but that hope is very much a passport to Dostoevsky's "underground." Anyway, since he could not accept *no* for an answer to the question of intrinsic order, he started looking for evidence of *yes.* And wanting to get this evidence from the horse's mouth, so to speak, he went to consult an ambassador of the Queen of Sciences, a mathematician.

If only he had never gone there! Their lengthy conversation cannot possibly be repeated here for, to start with, like most people in his field, the mathematician believed himself to be talking in the simplest, most evident terms which even a child would understand—without understanding that the other did not understand him. Several times our man tried to interrupt politely: He was not so much interested in the proof that the number of primes is infinite, but rather in the question whether mathematics offered clear and plain rules for arriving at correct decisions in practical life situations, or reliable laws for the prediction of future events. And now, at long last, the mathematician thought he had understood what the other wanted of him: But of course, these problems concerned a special domain of mathematics, namely probability theory and its application to statistics. For instance, on the strength of many years of data collection one could assume, with a probability bordering certainty, that the safety record of air traffic was 99.92 percent while a mere 0.08 percent of passengers lose their lives in aviation accidents. When our man now wanted to know which of the two percentages he personally belonged to, the mathematician lost patience and threw him out.

There is not much point in describing the

long, painful and expensive quest that our man embarked on, which brought him into contact with philosophy, logic, sociology, psychology, theology, some weird cults and other assorted world explanations of doubtful quality. The outcome was virtually the same as in the conversation with the mathematician: Every time there was a glimmer of hope that the discipline in question did have the final answer; but every time there then emerged some snag or complication which again postponed final certainty into some distant future—for instance, to the end of time, to the attainment of some higher level of consciousness, or to the occurrence of something nobody could predict would occur.

The only tangible result of this quest was that while, as already mentioned, our man had formerly embraced life with candid confidence and childlike innocence, he now became obsessed with security. And he himself found it puzzling that he should have managed to lead a secure and contented existence as long as he had given no thought to the certainty of security while he now felt increasingly unsafe and had to take practical precautions to ward off what seemed an ever-increasing number of dangers. Without going into detail, it may suffice to say that these were more than mere superstitious acts. We all know that such little tricks, like knocking on wood, are unreliable. But the preventions that our man developed worked without fail. They were absolutely reliable, perhaps due to the fact that the dangers which they were supposed to banish did not exist in the first place; for instance, the threat of malaria in Northern Greenland or those wild elephants roaming the forests of America which can be safely kept away by clapping one's hands every ten seconds. The trouble was that each of these measures protected our man only against *one* particular danger, while the number of imaginable dangers is countless. Just think how many other, quite possible perils remained unaffected by his security precautions.

And not only this. Our man's behavior perplexed other people. He found that friends and strangers reacted to him in increasingly odd ways the more he tried to make the world a safer place for all. People avoided him, mothers kept their children out of his way, and they whispered and laughed behind his back. This bothered him, increased his sense of insecurity, and made him behave with even more circumspection. The more he tried to protect himself, the more he felt himself in need of protection.

But even when other people did not affect him directly, the dangers still increased. For instance, he began to pay attention to the daily newspaper horoscopes. When he read predictions that were positive and enjoyable, they either did or did not come true. Their failure to materialize was disappointing, but did not represent any danger. The ominous predictions, on the other hand, somehow turned out, in comparison, to be more reliable. To give just one example: One morning, at breakfast, our man read that people born under his sign of the zodiac (approximately 330 million souls) should be especially careful on this particular day. The impact of this revelation made him spill his coffee, but this little mishap was obviously not serious enough to consider the danger as accounted for. He therefore decided to walk to work rather than take his car. Of course, walking is safer than driving, but every thirteenth step has its own dangers, to say nothing of the thirteenth step of a staircase. When he came to that step in a pedestrian underpass and tried to avoid it by jumping to the fourteenth, he stumbled and bruised his knee. So the horoscope was right after all.

Since our man had not received a classical education and had not (yet) been analyzed, he knew nothing of his famous ancestor, Oedipus Rex, whose parents had been told by the oracle of Delphi that Oedipus would kill his father and marry his mother. Whatever his parents did, and Oedipus as well, to escape this curse was exactly what was needed to fulfill the prophecy. (With hindsight, of course, we might say that the whole mess could have been avoided if his parents had thumbed their nose at the Pythia.)

But back to our man. The years passed, but not his problem. On the contrary, it only became more subtle and all-embracing, albeit in a certain sense more respectable. For security, pure and simple, no longer concerned him. Rather, there was a new feeling towards the world and his own life; he had a longing for something he vaguely called happiness, harmony, being in tune; something that he experienced in curious moments when he was incomprehensibly touched by music or seemingly quite trivial experiences. . . . At this point we shall leave him, temporarily, and return to him again at the end of the book. For in order to understand him better, we first must examine a number of other ultra-solutions.

2

Twice as Much Is Not Necessarily Twice as Good

"That Dr. Xylmurbafi really understands his business," Mr. Hypochond happily remarked to his wife. "I have taken this medicine for only one day, and already I feel much better." He had reason to be content, for his other doctors had been unable to bring about an improvement. So it was not surprising that he was anxious to speed up his recovery. But somewhat less obvious was the fact that this made him vulnerable to one of Hecate's oldest and most banal suggestions, namely the notion that twice as much has to be twice as good. So Mr.

Hypochond doubled his dose and last Thursday had to be admitted to the emergency ward of our local hospital.

So what, the reader may ask? What is so remarkable about this? To which one could reply that it is this very condescension that makes us blind to the danger of "twice as much." As far as medicines go, most of us are probably more intelligent than Mr. Hypochond. But beyond that we are not at all immune to this form of ultra-solution, as many a professional problem-solver has found out the hard way.

Let us take the example of what may be called the multiplication mania. What seems more logical than to assume that a solution, once found and successfully applied over and over again, must also lend itself to larger and larger problems? But one hundred times as much is one hundred times that much only in abstract mathematics. The trick that Hecate applies to these situations, and that leads to the most unexpected, "illogical" failures, occurs when she lets things flip from quantity to quality at the most crucial moment. And it is this jump that comes as a complete surprise to reason and common sense.

Cake every day makes us dislike cake; that seems obvious. That there should be a maximal span in bridge construction does not even surprise us lay people. At a certain point too much is simply too much.—But what, the reader may ask, has this got to do with *quality*, with turning into something *else*, rather than simply into more of the *same?* A few examples:

Many large corporations that not only produce already established products but are also engaged in the research and development of new or improved ones, pass through monotonously identical crises that all have to do with the problems caused by the idea of naïve enlargement and multiplication. The vicious cycle involved here usually runs somewhat like this: After long and expensive trials the scientists of the Research and Development Department have come up with the prototype of a fabulous new product, have tested it thoroughly and proudly turned it over to the production engineers. However, in their hands the new gadget turns out to have serious defects and thus is not marketable. Now the war starts between the two departments: "Surely, it is not asking too much to take this perfectly functioning macromicroparallelcompensator, as it stands here on the table in front of your very eyes, and mass-produce it," snort the Research and Development people. "It may function perfectly in your egg heads, but only there and not in the real world—here are the first five hundred of them, built exactly according to your specifications, and they are fit to be thrown out!" This is how the production experts see it.

What is so enjoyable for Hecate in these cases is that both parties are right *and* wrong at the same time. Five hundred MMP-compensators are not just many *more,* but quite *different* from the original one. In one similar case, for instance, it was found that the research department had utilized a small laboratory centrifugue in order to produce a certain emulsion, while the production engineers had built a huge, cubic mixer for the same purpose. But what came out of that tank did not have the same consistency as the mixture from the centrifugue. As a result of such a crisis, management may then resort to the ultra-solution of saving what still can be saved and turn to the production of spaghetti.

Too theoretical and too unconvincing? All right, here are two other case descriptions:

It is far less economical to ship the same quantity of crude oil in two small tank ships than in one tanker with double capacity. The doubling or even quintuplicating of tonnage thus seemed the self-evident, more-of-the-same, solution. But, much to the experts' surprise, more-of-the-same once again turned out to be something *else.* Over and above a certain tonnage, these floating giants begin to behave differently from their smaller ancestors. A number of tanker disasters during the last decades, in plain daylight and at calm sea, could be traced back to a difference in steering ability. Moreover, it was found that the tankers have the bad habit of blowing up at the least likely time, namely on their voyage *to* the loading terminals and while the crew is busy hosing down the *empty* holds with seawater.

The second example is perhaps even more illustrative: In order to protect their huge space rockets from weather conditions—mostly rain and lightning—the U.S. Space Agency decided to build an equally huge space-vehicle preparation hangar. Hangars have been built for the last eighty years or more, and all that needed to be done—so it seemed—was to multiply the dimensions of the largest existing hangars by a factor of maybe ten or more. As mentioned by John Gall in his most entertaining book *Systemantics* [4]*, it was found, probably again to the surprise of the experts, that an enclosed space of that size (after all, it is the largest construction on earth) has its own inner climate, namely clouds, rain, and discharges of static electricity—and thus produces from within itself the very phenomena it was supposed to protect against.

An essentially identical ultra-solution was resorted to by Monsieur and Madame Machin in the French Département Alpes-Maritimes, proving that Hecate's techniques work on large as well as small scales. The couple dearly wished to have children, but the years passed and their wish remained unfulfilled. And then, when they had almost abandoned all hope, the

---

*Figures in brackets refer to the bibliography at the end of the book.

wife became pregnant and in due course gave birth to a baby boy. The parents' joy was simply indescribable, so much that they wanted the child's name to reflect and glorify this blessing. After a long search and many deliberations they finally decided to call him *Formidable.* However, it soon turned out that this eccentric name was all the more ill-chosen as the boy grew up rather small and puny, and even as an adult continued to be the constant target of monotonous, brainless jokes about the discrepancy between his name and his physical appearance. Formidable suffered silently, but on his death bed he said to his wife: "All my life I have put up with this idiotic name, but I do not want it perpetuated on my gravestone. Write on it whatever you want, but do not mention my name." The wife promised, he died, and since their marriage had indeed been loving and harmonious, she eventually ordered a gravestone with the inscription: "Here lies a man who was always kind and faithful to his wife." Everybody who passed by the grave and read the inscription said: *"Tiens, c'est formidable."*

Whosoever has experienced—even if just once—this unexpected and unexpectable flipover of an attempted solution into more of the same problem will have little difficulty in drawing the wrong conclusion and falling into the trap of another ultra-solution which is the exact opposite of the one just described. This is our next subject.

3

Good Can Be Bad

Even more "logical" than the idea we just examined—that twice as much *must* be twice as good—is the naïve conclusion that if something is bad, its contrary must be good. Nobody seems to know for sure where this idea originated, but philosophers and scholars of religious history tend to attribute it to Mani (216–276 A.D.), founder of a gnostic religion, Manicheism, whose rapid growth for a while almost outpaced Christianity. It advocated a radical dualism, an irreconcilable antagonism between the forces of good and evil, between light and darkness, spirit and matter, God and the devil; a conflict that could be resolved only by the final and total victory of the spirit. But did our ancestors really have to wait for Mani in order to split the world into pairs of opposites? After all, Adam and Eve had already eaten from the Tree of so-called Knowledge and thereby started to distinguish good from evil, and even animals seem to do all right with this philosophy: Eating is good, hunger is bad, being eaten even worse—such is life and you don't have to be a philosopher to grasp this. So?

Unfortunately or—depending on your preference—fortunately it is not that simple. As an illuminating example, let us take the life history of an only seemingly fictitious character who quite seriously wanted to live by this Manichean philosophy of opposites. I define him as "only seemingly fictitious" because the reader will easily associate him with the names of many personalities in different parts of the world, and from the distant past up to the present. Let us give him the exotic name of *Ide Olog*.

There is not much to report of Olog's early life, except that he was a very sensitive child, although (or perhaps just because) his childhood had been remarkably free from unpleasant, sobering or even disappointing experiences, since his parents—belated believers in "permissive education"—had never demanded anything of him. As a result he was totally unprepared for what came crashing down upon him as he left the fool's paradise of his home. His calamity indeed resembled the biblical eviction from Eden, for like Adam and Eve, he, too, became conscious of the separation of our world into good and evil. But the important difference between Olog and our forefather was that Adam somehow managed to put up with the mess he found himself in, while Olog was enraged by what to him amounted to a sudden violation of his civil rights: the fact that his environment refused to tend to his every need, wish and whim. The world was out of joint, but unlike Hamlet, it was for him no cursed spite to think that he was born to put it right.

With this Olog placed himself on the recruitment list of Hecate and her witches. For just as the espionage services are constantly on the lookout for gamblers, drinkers, junkies, etc. who can easily be blackmailed, Hecate and her witches are always very interested in types who not only want to put the world *right*, but are intent on making it *happy*.

"Young Olog is really quite promising," said the first witch, who had been shadowing him for quite some time. "Just imagine, today at the post office he went into a rage when they told him in no uncertain terms to stand in line and await his turn just like everybody else. Now he sits in his room and broods."

"Ha, I love brooders," said the second witch,

"especially those who can be turned into fast breeders!"

Hecate was interested and asked her team for suggestions. Eventually they agreed on the following successful procedure.

First, they brain-washed Olog into the firm conviction that his view of the world was the only true and right one. To achieve this first goal was not too difficult, because Olog's mental range had about the width of a television screen, and he was thus spared the sobering realization that the ingenious solutions that are constantly rising above the eastern horizon, pristine and virginal, had already made a prior appearance at least forty years ago and had then been flushed down into that sewage treatment plant of ideas below the western horizon.

The witches' second step produced almost instant success. Olog was made to wonder why he alone was so clearly aware of all the evil in the world, while the others kept living their dull, passive existences and resigned themselves to the way things were. This had to be the doing of some sinister force, a force which . . . just a moment, let's see—yes, that had to be it: which *mystified* mankind! And now the phenomenon had a name—mystification—and since it had a name, it *was* a phenomenon, a real, verifiable, existing thing. Is anybody perhaps suggesting that there could exist names without the *thing* thus named? Names without substance, like those little angels in baroque paintings with only head and wings but no bodies? Oh no, the discovery of a name is the discovery of the *thing* itself. If this were not so, we would be in trouble, for what would we do without ether, phlogiston, earth rays, the influence of the planets, schizophrenia, phrenology, characterology, numerology?—And do you think that it was mere coincidence that the first and the last name of our hero eventually coalesced into the term *ideology?* But I am getting ahead of myself.

And who mystifies? Clearly those who have a vested interest in keeping the masses in their state of witless resignation toward the world's imperfection. In other words, those sinister powers that stand in the way of mankind's triumphant march into the terrestrial paradise. But who are they, and where? It is notoriously difficult to find somebody if you don't have the faintest idea of his whereabouts. By comparison it seems much easier to go about this business in reverse, to incite the masses and make them see the truth. Can you see how adeptly Olog already mastered this thinking by seeing the world in pairs of opposites: True and false; right and wrong; active and passive; free and unfree; happy and unhappy; and, above all; good and bad?

I do not want to be misunderstood: Olog was a Parsifal type, a guileless fool; he wanted true happiness, not just for a selected few, but for any and all—even and especially for those who were still unable or too dense to grasp the idea of his final solution. But with this he had reached that critical point at which not only more of the *same* turned into something *else*, but events acquired a momentum of their own and there was no longer an essential difference between Olog and Macbeth. Admittedly, Olog did not (yet) wade in blood, while Macbeth, on the other hand, was totally devoid of any missionary zeal. After all, he was not an ideologue, but "merely" a power-hungry, violent criminal, obsessed with the idea of getting away with it scot-free.

So how did it come about that Olog, in his idealism, finally did plant a time bomb in a crowded department store, killing several people and maiming many others?

At this point it becomes necessary to refer to something that I have so far left out of my exposition. Until now the reader may have been left with the impression that Hecate imposes her sinister ultra-solutions on a helpless and defenseless world which at best becomes aware of impending disaster when it is much too late to avert it. ". . . this idiocy,/the fire it's too late to extinguish,/called fate," as Max Frisch so aptly defines this calamity in his play *The Fire Raisers*. But there are individuals who somehow manage to anticipate Hecate's moves and to spoil her machinations. We shall meet at least a few of these wolves in sheep's clothing in the course of my case descriptions. One of them is the philosopher Hermann Lübbe who identified the process of "self-authorization to use violence," [10] thereby making Olog's act of terrorism appear less incomprehensible. For if someone who starts out as a voice crying in the wilderness, perhaps "sicklied o'er with the pale cast of thought," cannot find anybody to listen to him, his fantasies will sooner or later push him into the role of the surgeon whom Providence has called upon to apply the healing knife out of deep concern for mankind's ignorant suffering. And a surgeon, as we all know, has to cut, doesn't he? Or to put it even more prosaically: You have to break eggs to make an omelette.

To conclude his case, let me merely mention that there was only one thing that Olog himself found deeply puzzling, namely that his heroic act had a totally unforeseen effect. Rather than destabilizing the structure of established power and its odious mystifications, it horrified people to the extent that even those who otherwise disagreed on many social and political issues were united in their call for more of the existing order. It goes without saying that this totally unexpected result prompted Olog to engage in even more insane atrocities.

That much about Olog, the ideologue. Maybe the reader will see the case quite differently. Let me merely point out that some twenty-five hundred years ago Heraclitus, the great philosopher of change, warned that extreme deeds never lead to final victory, but only strengthen the opposite extreme. But who cares about Heraclitus? It is so much more noble and heroic to embrace a marvellous idea, totally and unconditionally, even if one's hands get dirty and fate soon knocks at the door (poompoom-poom-pumm . . .).

The witches, in any case, were jubilant. Once again they had succeeded in pulling off the basically ludicrous trick of utilizing that which is bad about goodness for their sinister purposes. With this, at long last, I am getting to the point I wanted to make: In the preceding chapter we saw that twice as much is not necessarily twice as good. Now we are beginning to suspect that the opposite of something bad is not necessarily good, but may be even worse. Into the all too rarified spirituality of classic Hellas burst the dark and chaotic frenzy of Dionysus; the exalted veneration of femininity in the cult of the Virgin Mary and in courtly love had as its road companion the unspeakable inhumanity of the witch hunts; for a while the religion of love relied on the Inquisition; the ideals of the French Revolution required the introduction of the guillotine; the Shah was followed by the Ayatollah; the Somozas by the Sandinistas; and in Saigon people may still be trying to decide who was worse, the liberators from across the Pacific or those from Hanoi.

Why? Because there is something fundamentally wrong in assuming that the opposite of bad must be good—and not just because the good is not yet good enough, or because the bad has not yet been totally exterminated.

> . . . I am perplexed by my own data, and my conclusion is in direct contradiction to the original idea with which I started. Starting from unlimited freedom, I arrived at unlimited despotism. I will add, however, that there can be no other solution of the social formula than mine . . .

This is how Dostoevsky's philanthropist Shigalev puts it in *The Demons*. And Berdyaev, who acknowledged Dostoevsky as one of his masters, had something similar to say about the ideal of freedom:

> . . . Freedom cannot be identified with goodness or truth or perfection: it is by nature autonomous, it is freedom and not goodness. [. . .] Any identification or confusion of freedom with goodness and perfection involves a negation of freedom and a strengthening of methods of compulsion; obligatory goodness ceases to be goodness by the fact of its constraint. [2]

"Sire, the striving for perfection is one of the worst maladies that can befall the human spirit," we read in an opening address of the French Senate to Napoleon I. For C. G. Jung, every psychological extreme contains "secretly its opposite, or stands in some sort of intimate and essential relation to it" [7]. And 2300 years before this, Lao-Tzu in the inimitable clarity of his style, describes the emergence of evil out of the very existence of the good, and *vice versa:*

When the great Tao is forgotten,
Kindness and morality arise.
When wisdom and intelligence are born,
The great pretense begins.

When there is no peace in the family,
Filial pity and devotion arise.
When the country is confused and in chaos,
Loyal ministers appear.

These are not explanations, but descriptions of one aspect of our world: He who would posit the *summum bonum* thereby also posits the *summum malum.* The uncompromising pursuit of whatever name is given to the supposedly highest ideal—be it security, patriotism, peace, freedom, happiness or whatever—is an ultra-solution, a force which, to paraphrase Goethe, always seeks the good and always creates evil.

But please, keep these thoughts to yourself if you live in certain countries, for otherwise you may end up in a "rehabilitation camp" or the peace fighters might bash your head in. . . .

4

The (Allegedly) Excluded Middle

Perhaps I am exaggerating, and things are not quite so dangerous. But there is little doubt that the Manichean world, the world that is neatly divided into pairs of opposites, would not be half so neat if there were more people like Franzi Wokurka, resident of Steinhof, a small town in Austria. Franzi's trials and tribulations—for they are our next subject—reached their peak when he was about thirteen years old. He was standing in the town's Beethoven Park, in front of a large flower bed, and there discovered a sign with the inscription "No trespassing." This brought back a problem that had been bothering Franzi more and more during recent years. Once again he found himself in a situation that seemed to present only two possibilities, and both were unacceptable. *Either* he exerted his freedom in the face of this oppressive prohibition and began trampling on the flowers, at the same time risking arrest; *or* he stayed off the flower bed. But the mere thought of being such a coward, of obeying a stupid sign, made his blood boil. For a long time he stood there, undecided, at his wit's end, until suddenly, maybe because he had never looked at flowers long enough, something totally and completely different came to his mind: *These flowers are beautiful.*

Do you find this story trivial? If so, I can only say: Young Wokurka did not see it that way. That realization swept over him like a wave that lifts you up and swiftly, effortlessly carries you along. He was now aware that the world could perhaps be seen in a totally different, entirely new way. *I* want this flower bed just the way it is; *I* want this beauty; *I* am my own law, my own authority; he kept saying to himself over and over again. And suddenly that "no trespassing" sign had lost all its importance; the pitfall of the Manichean opposites, "submission or rebellion and nothing else" had vanished. Of course, Franzi's euphoria did not last, but something fundamental was changed; there now was a faint melody in him, often quite inaudible, but sometimes clear enough just when he seemed about to sink again into the morass of *either-or*. For instance, when he learned to drive he always buckled up his seat belt, because *he* had decided that this was a reasonable thing to do. And when shortly afterwards the great public debate arose about the government's right to mandate the use of safety belts, he could not have cared less about all the hullabaloo. He stood *outside* the controversy.

Later Franzi began seriously and systematically to explore this outlook on life. If we give free rein to our imagination, we can picture him no longer capable of understanding the simplistic logic of the biblical maxim, "Whosoever is not for me is against me." When he tried to figure it out, he felt like that man of whom the judge asks, "Have you stopped beating your wife? Answer yes or no!" and threatens him with a charge of contempt because—having *never* beaten her—he *cannot* answer either *yes* or *no*. This sort of bind now seemed to Franzi like a bad dream, and the comparison actually makes good sense, for whatever one tries to do in a nightmare—running, hiding, fighting back—does not free the dreamer from his dream. The solution to a nightmare is waking up, but awakening is no longer a *part* of the dream, is not more of the same, but is something entirely different, something *outside* the dream.

Later, at the university, Franzi learned that this "basically different, outside thing" wreaks havoc even in formal logic, except that there it is called "the excluded middle." As in the Bible quotation above, classic logic postulates that any assertion must either be true or false and that there is no such thing as a third possibility *(tertium non datur).* But then there came that *enfant terrible,* that classic liar who said: I am lying. If it was true that he was lying, he had told the truth; but then his statement, "I am lying," was a lie. And in the second half of the twentieth century, over two thousand years after the liar's appearance, what do we make of the statement "The King of France is bald"? True or false?

"People like that Wokurka bloke can make you hate your work," bitched the second witch. "You spend a lot of time and energy constructing what seems like a fool-proof situation with only two possibilities, both ultra-solutions, and he somehow finds a third and walks away. For instance, I give him only the choice between cowardice and foolhardiness, and he chooses courage. I try to make him lust for something so that he may begin to dread the possibility of not attaining it, and he is indifferent to the one and to the other. Recently I tried to get other people to force him into saying whether or not he believed in God—and he simply shrugged and quoted Kant, Comte and Spencer (whoever they are), who maintain this is no problem, for *if* God existed, his existence could not be grasped by the human mind. Therefore, according to Wokurka, this eternal bickering between believers and atheists is a pseudo-problem; he considers himself an agnostic.

I even know that back in 1942, when Wokurka was still in his youth, there was already clear clear evidence of this malicious character defect. Remember, things were then beginning to go badly for our beloved pupil Adolf von Braunau who, with his unusual talent for ultra-solutions, had the ingenious idea of printing posters with the question: *National Socialism or Bolshevik Chaos?* Now, don't you think that even the most stupid person would understand that he had to choose between the blond, blue-eyed forces of salvation and the diabolical forces of evil? What did Wokurka do? He glued little stickers to those posters: *Spuds or Potatoes?* And weren't our friends livid that somebody was making fun of their official and final definition of good and evil! He was playing with his life, but I think that even as a suicide candidate he's a disappointment. That man is capable of coming up with something else if we give him the choice of continuing to suffer or killing himself. No doubt about it, he's dangerous—let's blacklist him."

"Fair enough," said Hecate. "but you seem to forget that we've been up against such types for as long as I can remember. Recall what happened in 1334, when the lord of Hochosterwitz

Castle made us look idiotic. Not only us, but the Duchess of Tyrol, Margareta Maultasch, who besieged the lord's castle. The defenders were down to one ox and two bags of barley when they were faced with the decision to starve or surrender. And what did they do? Every child knows the story: They did not choose the one *or* the other, but slaughtered the ox, stuffed it full of the last barley and threw it over the ramparts right in front of Margareta's encampment. So the Duchess thought: What's the point of continuing the siege if they have so much to eat they can let me have some? And off she marched. How the people in the castle laughed! Of course they were Austrians, all of them, just like Franzi Wokurka. These Irrelevanters of the West, as one of them himself said. For them the situation is always hopeless, but not serious."

So the excluded middle, the *tertium*, seems to exist after all. But it probably lives in seclusion, in the shadow of common sense, which, as we know, tends to divide the world neatly and reliably into irreconcilable opposites. Lao-Tzu, using still another phrase, referred to the *tertium* as the Great Sense. The trouble here, however, is that Great Sense has a direct opposite, the Great Nonsense. Could this be the reason why in certain religions God must not be named?

5

A "Chain Reaction" of Kindness?

From the foregoing, it becomes fairly clear that the witches do not know very much about logic and metaphysics. But even when they're trying to mess up less esoteric matters they frequently find themselves up against some unexpected but by no means unexpectable difficulties.

A typical example was the odd change that took place in the life of Amadeo Cacciavillani who lived in the town of Finimondo, way to the southeast of Florence. Signor Cacciavillani was the living example of what in the mathematical theory of games is called a zero-sum player. This had nothing to do directly with the fact that he was Italian, for there are zero-sum players everywhere in the world—even in the White House and the Kremlin.

(The term *zero-sum game* refers to that class of games whose simplest example is a bet between two people. What the one person loses (e.g. fifty dollars) the other wins. Gain (plus fifty) and loss (minus fifty), added together, give the sum of zero dollars. In other words, gain and loss are inseparably linked; the one is unthinkable without the other.)

To be a zero-sum player means to embrace, fully and invariably, the Manichean thesis that in *all* life situations there are *only* two possibilities: winning or losing. Once again, there is no third possibility. (Or, as a joker once remarked, the world is filled with two types of people: Those who think that there are two types of people, and those who don't.)

This zero-sum philosophy has always been preached in military academies and similar institutions, although in fairness it should be mentioned that certain exceptions were made until about two hundred years ago. For example, the word of honor of an enemy general was considered absolutely trustworthy. But since those distant days we have successfully outgrown such superstitious assumptions.

Hecate pursues the indoctrination of young people into the zero-sum game relentlessly and in various ways. I have already made honorable mention of the military. Special acknowledgment is due also to sports coaches and their insistence on the overriding importance of winning (accompanied by instantaneous action, again untainted by the pale cast of thought) and the disgrace of defeat. Finally, there is scarce need for special reference to the ennobling effects of the mass media with their glorification of power and winning by any means, fair or foul.

In Cacciavillani this philosophy had found its almost perfect incarnation. He lived for winning in all aspects of his life, and therefore he lived in constant fear of losing or being taken advantage of. Thus his philosophy was simple, though uncomfortable, for to live in a perennial state of alert can fray even the toughest nerves and irritate the thickest skin. It goes without saying that as a by-product of his permanent fear of losing, he heartily enjoyed other people's misfortunes. (Does the reader perhaps feel that he knows Signor Cacciavillani rather well?) And finally there was something else, obvious to everybody except Cacciavillani: His constant aggressive and defensive postures *created* the very situations against which he perpetually tried to protect himself, and this again confirmed his view that life was a never-ending battle. The magic power of a zero-sum game lies in the fact that it imposes its rules on virtually everybody—

whether the others themselves want to play zero-sum or not.

So much by way of introducing Cacciavillani and zero-sum. Now, about a year and a half ago, on a gloomy winter morning, he parked his car on a side street at a certain distance from his office. After having walked about five hundred feet he heard rapid footsteps behind him and then an unfamiliar voice said, "You left your car lights on." Without waiting for a response, the stranger turned around and quickly walked away.

Cacciavillani's first reaction—how could it be otherwise?—was to ask himself: What is he trying to do to me? What is he up to? But the stranger did not seem to have any further interest in him and had already disappeared among the crowd of people hurrying to work. Cacciavillani stood there, trying to make sense out of what had happened. Perhaps it would be more correct to say that he felt like a scientist who has just seen something through his telescope, under his microscope, or in his test tube which totally contradicts established theory.

"Why would this man run after me, to tell me, a total stranger, that I have forgotten to switch off the lights?" And Cacciavillani remembered how *he* had occasionally noticed cars with their lights on and how the thought of the owner finding himself late at night with an empty car battery had brought a spark of malicious joy into his otherwise joyless existence.

A "Chain Reaction" of Kindness?

What Cacciavillani did not yet know was that the stranger's decency had imposed upon him the rules of quite another game. But while walking back to his car, deep in thought, he had a vague feeling of obligation that was totally new to him, of obligation toward any other human being in a similar predicament. Not much came of it for a while. But then, months later, a decisive event did occur. He found a wallet with quite a bit of money in it, probably the owner's weekly pay. At first he rubbed his hands with joy at this windfall. But then, just then, the stranger who had run after him came to his mind, and that somehow spoiled it. He stared at the money, the *Carta d'identità,* a few old snapshots—and he thrust it all in his briefcase, got into his car and drove to the other side of the town of Finimondo. The owner of the wallet lived in a shabby house and at first could not believe his luck when Cacciavillani handed him the wallet, briefly explained where he had found it and then (to his own great surprise) even found pleasure in refusing the reward the owner offered him, it must be said without excessive enthusiasm.

As luck would have it, the owner of the wallet was himself an inveterate zero-sum player. "Fantastic," he said to himself, "I would never have thought that I would get my wallet back. But I must admit, I would never be so stupid as to return any money that I found . . ." He was wrong, for he could not know that it was now

Cacciavillani's turn to impose the rules of that strange game on another person, and when a comparable situation arose in *his* life, he, too, was "so stupid."

The point of the story? The stranger had triggered a chain reaction which did not end with Cacciavillani or the man with the wallet, but continued and spread in spite of numerous relapses by all concerned. Cacciavillani himself, even began to like this kind of winning and "power" over others.

Only the witches did not like it.

6

Nonzero-Sum
Games

The Hecate-team had reason to be disgusted. It happens again and again that even senior zero-sum players eventually get tired of pursuing that ultra-solution, and defect. The cases mentioned so far are not even the worst. In a very real sense Cacciavillani, for instance, did continue to play zero-sum in that he enjoyed feeling victorious by imposing his newly discovered "power" on others. But this is the exception rather than the rule. The idea of power never occurs to most people who get caught up in such a chain reaction of kindness.

If the reader is not quite convinced by these cases or finds them irrelevant, perhaps some examples from documented history will set any doubts to rest.

Until the bombing of Hiroshima, war, too, was considered a zero-sum game, since the territory lost by one state was the gain of the "victor." Little did it matter that millions of people might lose their lives in the process for, after all, they died as heroes *(dulce et decorum est pro patria mori)*, and the real belligerents more often died in retirement than on the battlefield. But so far as dying a hero's death goes, it is not everybody's preference. I mean not only one's own death but inflicting this honor on another human being—even if he wears a uniform of a different color. In Flanders, one of the major battlefields of World War I, amidst mud, despair, poison gas, blood and death, there arose, spontaneously and without any human planning, something that the British historian Tony Ashworth [1] described and documented as "the live and let live system." Ashworth found that neither side was excessively drawn to the idea of defeating the other. The mere fact that a soldier on one side had to endure these inhumane battlefield conditions passively, just as did the enemy, and at the same time was expected to contribute to them actively, paralyzed the zero-sum thinking that should inspire every good soldier. It was not rare for the enemy trenches to be no more than fifteen yards from one's own dugout, and it would have been easy to decimate one another with hand grenades. Not only did this *not* happen for weeks on end, but the two sides developed what can only be called friendly feelings for each other, especially during the Christmas season. According to Ashworth, "several forms of truce occurred throughout the trench war" and sometimes took on "the form of overt fraternisation on a widespread scale." (p. 24) Gradually there emerged quite specific, but nonetheless spontaneous non-aggression rituals, respected by both sides, such as the mutual avoidance of patrols in the midst of No-Man's-Land. Here is the description of one such encounter from Ashworth's interview material:

. . . we suddenly confronted, round some mound or excavation, a German patrol. We were perhaps twenty yards from each other, fully visible. I waved a weary hand, as if to say: what is the use of killing each other? The German officer seemed to understand, and both parties turned and made their way back to their own trenches. Reprehensible conduct, no doubt. (p.104)

And bloody right he was. On both sides the higher echelons became increasingly worried about this rapid decline in fighting spirit and soldierly discipline. In February 1917, for instance, the officer commanding the sixteenth British Infantry Division tried to stem this epidemic of friendly feelings by issuing an order that stated:

> The Divisional Commander wishes it to be clearly understood by all ranks that any understanding with the enemy of any description is strictly forbidden. No communication is to be held with him and any attempt on his part to fraternise is to be instantly repressed. In the event of any infringement disciplinary action is to be taken. (p. 37)

It is not too far-fetched to assume that, at least in theory, this must have brought the enemy high commands closer to each other in their shared worries about the rapid spread of the live-and-let-live epidemic. Had the commander of the German division facing the British sixteenth known of his colleague's order, he would probably have approved of it from the bottom of his heart (or whatever was left of it). In other words, an absurd situation had arisen which would have made it reasonable and desirable for the two commanding officers to take *joint* action to ward off this development. Of course, things never reached that point. But as we see, there seem to be no potential limits to the entanglements inherent in such situations.

The other consequence of this attempted solution is probably even more interesting to any student of the science of ultra-solutions. The official prohibition of the live-and-let-live system placed the soldiers in the trenches into a Manichean dilemma. *Either* they obeyed orders and fired at the enemy whenever and wherever he could be spotted, but in doing so exposed themselves to immediate retaliation for breaking the silent non-aggression pact. *Or,* they continued to respect the pact, but then risked court martial.

The untenability of the situation again led to the spontaneous emergence of a *tertium.* It was the rediscovery of an excellent solution dating back to the days of the Spanish colonists in the Western Hemisphere. The *conquistadores* and their successors found themselves constantly faced with senseless orders, issued by the Escorial in total ignorance of the actual situation. They soon began to react to them with the maxim *"se obedece pero no se cumple"* (one obeys, but does not comply). In Flanders, during World War I, the analogous solution proved eminently successful: One obeyed the order to shoot, but carefully avoided hitting the enemy—who, in turn, gratefully did likewise.

Something going beyond the live-and-let-live principle begins to emerge from the preliminary results of a large-scale study which two psychologists [3] began in 1981. They are interviewing non-Jews who had rescued Jews from extermination by the Nazis, often at great risk to themselves and perhaps just as often without even knowing the ones who were rescued personally. When asked why they had done this, many rescuers tend to react almost instinctively with the counter-question, "What do you mean?" and, and when the question is repeated, are likely to reply almost with embarrassment, "It was the right thing to do," or "I was only doing what a human being should do for another human being."

Admittedly, these are exceptional people, yet they are not as rare as one might think. One can find them everywhere, in private as well as in public life, wherever people depend on one another not only for survival but also for comfort, and—unlikely as it may seem—even in foreign policy matters. Underlying their outlook on life is a different set of rules. In terms of game theory they play *nonzero-sum games,* that is, games in which the loss of one player is not necessarily the gain of the other. Rather, *both* can win or lose. A nuclear war would be the prime example of a nonzero-sum game, of an ultra-solution which would lead to total disaster. But the very opposite is also possible. Through mutual concessions and other forms of meeting each other half-way (actions which any red-blooded zero-sum player would of course consider "defeats") there may be advantages for *all* players which none of them could have reached individually.

It goes without saying that true ideologues who are firmly committed to their ultra-solutions of world improvement are immune to these processes. Any offer by the other party to negotiate or to make concessions is either seen as nothing but a clumsy trap, or diagnosed as a sign of weakness that must be exploited immediately in order to fortify one's own position. And when, as a result of this reaction, the other party is forced back into an adversary position, this "proves" clearly how right one's suspicions had been from the beginning. And what matters even more: To enter into the spirit of a *nonzero-sum game* would be tantamount to betraying the sacred ideology.

In the field of international relations the incompatibility of zero-sum and nonzero-sum games is what the tensions between East and West are mostly about. The French historian and author Jean-François Revel immediately comes to mind in this connection, even though he does not use game-theoretical terms. In his lecture in Bonn on October 25, 1984 [16] and especially in his book *How Democracies Perish* [15] he sees the fundamental difference between democratic and totalitarian governments in the willingness of the former to negotiate and in what I just called the zero-sum philosophy of the latter. The foreign policy of our democracies is determined by their domestic policy, whose primary concern is the security and prosperity of their citizens. Therefore, to use Revel's formulation, foreign policy democracies strive to achieve "a state of equilibrium that corresponds to their inner equilibrium." Totalitarianism, on the other hand, bases itself on an ideology, on a final and therefore compulsory definition of the human, societal and even scientific reality of our world. Hence—and here I quote Revel again—for totalitarian governments "the mere existence of different systems is incompatible with their security."

One might add that for this reason the foreign policy of totalitarian states has one and only one goal, namely uncompromising, final and world-wide victory, for only this ultra-solution can put an end to their *zero-sum game* and establish the terrestrial Paradise. Of course, this strategy does not exclude verbose, tactical avowals of appeasement which rarely fail to convince western citizens and their governments that the other side has now joined the *nonzero-sum game*. (For some strange reason, in addition to *Munich* the city of *Helsinki* also comes to mind in this connection.)

Nonzero-sum players are devoid of messianic fervor; even if they are motivated by the most selfish considerations they still believe in the live-and-let-live principle as the best strategy. Thus, in dealing with one another the western powers, to quote Revel once more,

> strive to reach ever new compromises whose average value is the most advantageous common denominator for all of them. [. . .] All democratic diplomacy presumes that it pays to make conces-

sions because the opponent, of whom it is assumed that he is reasonable and moderate, will thereby be motivated to take these concessions into account and to counter them with concessions of his own, thereby contributing to the reaching of a lasting compromise. [16]

A utopia? Not at all, at least not where nonzero-sum players achieve compromises rather than ultra-solutions. It may sound incredible to younger people, but thanks to what had been hammered into our heads in the first half of this century, we "knew" that France and Germany were mortal enemies for all eternity and that terrible wars between them every thirty years were determined by the laws of historic process. We believed it just as we now believe that the hatred between the Arab states and Israel or the bloodshed in Northern Ireland cannot be avoided. And yet, on June 22, 1963, two presidents who were not otherwise known for unusual statesmanship managed to sign a friendship treaty that climaxed a rapid change in the relations between their two countries. Anybody who still stood ready to defend the *Vaterland* or *la douce France* against the archenemy on the other side of the Rhine could be considered a political dinosaur.

7

Brave Digitalized World

According to an old joke, making its tired rounds in anthropology departments, the missing link between *apes* and *homo sapiens* has at long last been discovered. It turns out to be *man* . . .

The joke is unfortunately not just a joke, and right now we are indeed that missing link. But it is only a question of time until we shall be *sapiens* (replete with sagacity). A glorious future has already begun, an ultra-solution into which Hecate will make us slide comfortably and almost without noticing it.

Even a superficial examination of human history makes it evident that all evil can be traced back to human irrationality. Madness, frenzy, delusion, envy, fear, greed and all sorts of other passions are the reasons why the world is as unpleasant as it is. Why can't everybody be as reasonable as I myself am?

The trouble is that everybody, myself included, has a brain in which the centers concerned with reason and logic (the "science of correct thinking") are sitting on top of the so-called limbic system which we inherited from our reptilian ancestors and which never evolved past crude instincts and emotions. And this is why we have not yet arrived at the state of *homo sapiens.*

But, as already mentioned, this nuisance is about to be corrected. I'm not referring to extraterrestrial beings who might be at work to knock sense and reason into our planet, but to foolproof and unemotional contraptions put together by the earthlings we call human.

There are people who are worried about this utopia and its predictable consequences. The worry found its literary expression as early as 1950 in a novel by the Rumanian author Virgil Gheorghiu, entitled *The 25th Hour.* [5] According to one of the book's main characters, the poet Traian, this is "the hour when mankind is beyond salvation—when it is too late even for the coming of the Messiah. It is one hour past the last hour." And Traian predicts what the first symptom of this terminal illness will be:

> A society which contains millions of millions of mechanical slaves and a mere two thousand million humans—even if it happens to be the humans who govern it—will reveal the characteristics of its proletarian majority. [. . .] In order to make use of their mechanical slaves men are obliged to get to know them and to imitate their habits and laws. [. . .] Conquerors, when they are numerically inferior to the conquered, will almost always adopt the language and customs of the occupied nation, for the sake of convenience or for other practical reasons—and that in spite of the fact that they are the masters.—The same process is working itself out in our own society, even though we are unwilling to recognize it. We are learning the laws and the jargon of our slaves, so that we can give them orders. And so, gradually and imperceptibly, we are renouncing our human qualities and our own laws. We are dehumanizing ourselves by adopting the way of life of our slaves. *The first symptom of this dehumanization is contempt for the human being.* (Italics mine.)

Any clear-minded, modern thinker would, of course, say that these are the words of a poet coming from the pen of a writer and thus hardly an expression of rationality. For these people, reason has little importance; they simply love to wallow in their vague, emotional, illogical unreality whose archaic laws (if one can speak of laws at all) defy objective definition, order, evaluation and measurement.

At the time Gheorghiu wrote his novel, the mechanical slave that comes closest to his description—the computer—was probably still shrouded in military secrecy, or carefully hidden in university departments. Perhaps Gheorghiu thought more in terms of the effect that the use of tools generally has upon those who create and use them. Metal workers are known to be more inclined to approach problems with an iron fist than by organizing tea parties; the number of British bank managers who in their spare time translate Homer's creations into impeccable English has probably dwindled to zero; and so far as I know, Dvořak was the only butcher who turned to composing immortal symphonies.

However, in the last forty years the computer has invaded not only the world of science, but also our entire society. Above all it has brought about an astronomical increase in our ability to manipulate numbers. Mathematical problems whose computation would have kept dozens of people busy for many months are now solved in fractions of a second. For example, to illuminate this quantum leap: When the first large computer (with the pretty name of ENIAC) was switched on at the University of Pennsylvania in 1946, it *doubled* the computing capacity of our planet. And compared with modern main frame computers, ENIAC was a Neanderthaler.

It is generally known that computers carry out both mathematical and logical operations. In other words, they are capable of drawing logical conclusions. In either case the computer's answers are erroneous only when there is some human error in the information that is fed into the machine. In computer jargon this complication is called GIGO (*g*arbage *i*n, *g*arbage *o*ut), meaning that from erroneous data one gets erroneous results. But by now GIGO has a second, more insidious meaning, namely "Gospel in, Gospel out." And this is where it gets interesting for our considerations: What we may only believe or hope to be true and correct comes back as eternal truth once it has passed through the computer's digestive system.

The magical concept underlying the hope of eventually arriving at a totally objective comprehension of the world, of reducing all its phenomena to the crystal-clear dimensions of numbers, is called *digitalization.* It is that language, composed only of the digits zero and one, in which one has to talk to comrade computer in order to make him accept the particular information he is supposed to juggle. The idea of being able to embrace and reveal the ultimate nature of reality in this way is reminiscent of Lord Acton's famous claim: Everything that exists, exists in a quantity and can therefore be measured.

However, this approach does not consider that there is also another, totally different language, namely the language of *analogy*—a term defined by Webster as a likeness in one or more ways between things otherwise unlike. Thus, an analogy is not the expression of a measurement, is not quantitatively identical with the measured object, but is related to its *quality*. And there is increasing awareness, even in the "hard" sciences, that quantity is only *one* aspect of quality. We have already seen in Chapter 2 how the former can inadvertently change into the latter, how *more of the same* can become something *else*. What concerns us here is the deplorable fact that, at least for the time being, certain undeniable qualities of human existence stubbornly refuse to let themselves be digitalized and reduced to the orderly world of zeros and ones. Sensations and emotions, for one thing, but then there is the entire sloppy, orphic, illusionary, dark, unreasonable, indefinable world of colors and scents, which is either totally beyond explanation or is the creative stuff of poets and artists. Consider the effect of a fiery sunset, the eyes of a cat or the sound of a piano concerto. All this and much more will have to digitalized until at long last we reach that brave new *World of Zero and One* [8] and the bell will toll the "25th hour."

And, besides, is it not much simpler to establish a viable relation with a computer than with another human being? The computer is not moody, is absolutely honest, makes no mistakes, and never argues. In return it only demands lucid rationality for which it generously rewards you. Just take a look at the Kafkaesque world of computer apprentices, long lines of them sitting in their cubicles in front of the computer screens, experiencing a kind of religious ecstasy when the Sphinx grants them absolution from all sins because they have hit the right keys. Who could blame them for impatiently awaiting that ultra-solution, that glorious day when the analogic will be exorcised even from their private lives because humans will finally obey only digital laws?

But until the bell finally tolls Gheorghiu's "25th hour" we can find temporary solace and reassurance in the computer's cousin, that other miracle of digitalization, the television set. Amazingly, Cicero already knew about television and its effects. In the year 80 B.C. he wrote:

> If we are forced, at every hour, to watch or listen to horrible events, this constant stream of ghastly impressions will deprive even the most delicate among us of all respect for humanity.

Of course, these effects are hidden behind a mask of grinning inanity. As far as that goes, Neil Postman [13] has said just about everything that needs to be said about how we can *amuse ourselves to death.* The basic idea of his book (itself most amusing) is that what we are facing is not an Orwellian *1984* future of oppression, but a "brave new world" in Aldous Huxley's sense—one in which "people will come to love their oppression, to adore the technologies that undo their capacity to think." For Postman, television is making the world into a culture obsessed with trivialities and ultimate emptiness.

In addition to Postman, the French sociologist Jean Baudrillard must be mentioned. In his lectures—admittedly with less pep and gallow's humor than Postman—he points to the *obscenity* of television, thus coming much closer to Cicero's concern. What he means by *obscene* may not be our common definition of the term. Primarily he is referring to the brutalizing effect of those pools of blood, those pictures of accident victims and violent crimes that have become the essential—if not the sole—ingredient of so-called newscasts, and especially to the shameless and disrespectful close-ups of people in desperate and tragic emergencies: The mother with the body of her dead child; the face of a dying man; the moronic questions shot at someone who has just escaped death by a hair's breadth and needs nothing more than quiet and composure. This voyeuristic display, this lack of the most elementary respect for human suffering and privacy, does indeed deserve to be called obscene (especially when followed immediately by the idiotic patter of a commercial). Of course, we all know and deeply appreciate that this is the way the mass media try to accomplish their sublime and yet democratic mission of keeping the citizenry fully informed. . . .

And for this reason the whole shebang lends itself egregiously to the implantation of ultra-solutions in hundreds of millions of brains.

8

"I Know Exactly What You Are Thinking"

"If I did not specialize in curses myself, I would have to say: What a cursed mess!" Hecate complained during a recent strategy session in her villa on the Mediterranean. "Why is it, despite all our efforts to convince people that their view of reality is the only possible and correct one, and any other view the result of madness or badness, and (above all) that they know exactly what goes on in other people's heads and consequently need not check out these assumptions—why is it, I say, that there is always some doubting Thomas who can't be convinced that he is absolutely right?"

Of course, Hecate was correct, except perhaps even she under-rated the importance of the "I-know-exactly-what-you-are-thinking" formula when she was planning her ultra-solutions. Let us therefore take a closer look at this phenomenon, and at a certain Mr. Mac-Nab, a physicist, from the city of Santa Cupertina in the Sillyclone Valley of Fornicalia. One day Mr. MacNab hit upon a brilliant idea which, because of my total ignorance of the field, I cannot describe even in the most superficial terms. Mind you, MacNab had had unusual ideas since childhood, but this time he hit the jackpot, and the idea became reality. He managed to build the machine, literally in his garage, and then test and market it. He was successful beyond all expectations and the purchase orders came pouring in.

Aha, the reader will think, this author is going to pontificate again about twice as much not being twice as good. Not at all. Thanks to his really unusual technical abilities, MacNab managed to foresee and avoid this complication. With him, the witches had to proceed differently. For not only did MacNab's sales increase, but problems of a purely administrative nature escalated; complications related to a voluminous correspondence, to bookkeeping, working out a realistic budget, and the like. So far, MacNab had dealt with these annoying necessities in a very marginal way, in his spare time, so to speak (between one and three o'clock in the morning), but now they were beginning to demand too much of his time. An administrator was needed. And Mac-Nab found himself one, even a very capable one. With this solution his decline began.

Because Mr. Muckerzan, the new man, was such an unusually capable and experienced administrator, tensions soon began to build up between the two men. MacNab, the brilliant inventor, whose successes were largely due to his innate ability to rise above ingrained thinking patterns and look at old problems in a totally new way, was what in modern brain research [19] is called a "right-hemispheric" personality. (According to these studies, the right half of our brain is characterized by the ability to grasp complex relationships and patterns, by an intuitive talent to perceive totalities.) And now MacNab found himself forced to collaborate closely with a man whose world was a painstakingly exact mosaic composed of equally painstakingly exact details.

"Muckerzan is driving me insane," MacNab raged while his wife listened patiently. "How can anybody lose himself so completely in minutiae? He does not see the forest for the trees, he is without the slightest understanding of what really matters, he is stuck in his world of figures and rules and legalistic trivia. And to top it off, he thinks I am irresponsible and a threat to the future of our business, I who have created this firm from nothing!"

At that very moment, Muckerzan was curs-
ing MacNab in the privacy of his apartment: "I
can't stand it anymore. Digitalize him—that's
what should be done with MacNab. For him,
simple facts don't exist. He can't see the trees
for the forest. One day he thinks this way, the
next day that way. I have no idea how he ar-
rives at his conclusions. But he expects me to
find them logical and excellent, and then to put
them into practice. A genius like him can't be
bothered with everyday matters; that sort of
thing can be left to narrow-minded sticklers
like me . . ."

As we can see, Mr. Muckerzan was "left
hemispheric." (The main function of the left
half of our brain appears to be the careful per-
ception and collection of objective details, and
their eventual integration into a mosaic-like to-
tality.)

The only thing that the two men had in common was their total inability to realize that the
other was not necessarily *wrong,* but was
thinking *differently.* For they were both right,
each in his own way, and so they continued to
rely blindly on ultra-solutions of the "I-am-
right-and-you-are-wrong" sort until the firm
went bankrupt.

As the reader may know from personal experience, this pattern is by no means limited to
work situations, but is a frequent problem between men and women. I gratefully recall an

analogy that one of my professors used in his lectures. A man, he explained, can be likened to an ellipse, which has two foci. The professor called one of these *logos,* meaning not only the realm of reason, but also the area of objectivity, professional and scientific matters and, even more generally, the world "out there." The other focus was *eros,* that is, the world of relations to another *human* being. At any given moment a man can be in only *one* of these foci. This is not a particular problem for a man; depending on the necessities of the situation, he simply goes back and forth between *logos* and *eros.*

A woman, on the other hand, can be likened to a circle. A circle can be viewed as a special case of an ellipse, one in which the two foci coincide. For a woman it is therefore perfectly natural to be in the *eros* and the *logos* mode *at the same time.* However, neither the woman nor the man has the slightest reason to assume that the partner has a different mental architecture that makes him/her act and react very differently. Here is a practical example, secretly recorded by the witches, who took great delight in the exchange:

WIFE: This cake doesn't seem to be rising.

HUSBAND: Perhaps not enough baking powder—what does the recipe say?

WIFE: That's typical of you!

HUSBAND: What's typical of me?

WIFE: You know exactly what I mean. You always do this and you know it gets on my nerves.

HUSBAND: What are you talking about? You say the cake isn't rising; I say it may not have enough baking powder—and all of a sudden we're not talking about baking powder, but some character defect of mine or God knows what. . . .

WIFE: Obviously, baking powder matters more to you than I do. I could have figured out about the baking powder myself—but it doesn't matter to you that I want you to enjoy this cake.

HUSBAND: I'm not denying this for a minute and I'm glad you want to bake a cake for me. I was only talking about baking powder, not about you.

WIFE: It's amazing how you men manage to keep things so compartmentalized! You make a woman feel all shivery!

HUSBAND: The real problem is how you women manage to make baking powder into a measure of love!
(And so on.)

"Why can't a woman be more like a man?" an exasperated Professor Higgins asks in Shaw's *Pygmalion*. No ready quotation comes to mind for the reverse, i.e., women complaining about men, but one can imagine that it would go something like this: I am important to you only when you happen to have time for me or when you can fit me into your other activities.

In this connection, a special Hecate trick deserves mention. It, too, can poison relations between the sexes or, for that matter, any interpersonal situation. It is the difference between *understanding* and *agreeing.* To treat these two concepts as if they meant the same thing is bound to lead to conflict. Only those on Hecate's blacklist appreciate that one can very well *understand* the partner's viewpoint without necessarily *agreeing* with it.

Sometimes it is claimed that men and women speak different languages. But as Oscar Wilde put it so elegantly when he was speaking of England and America, they are *separated* by a *common* language. Or, to put it still another way, the use of the same language produces the illusion that my partner must see reality as it really is—which is the way *I* see it. And if it turns out that the other person does not see it my way, this is clear evidence of madness or badness.

In an article several years ago, the Swiss professor Ernst Leisi presents an amusing example taken from John Locke's *Essay on Human Understanding:*

A group of distinguished British physicians were arguing at length whether a *liquor* is flowing inside the nerves. They were of divided opinion. The most diverse arguments were brought forth and agreement seemed almost impossible. At this point Locke asked for the floor and wanted to know if everybody was quite sure what was meant by the term *liquor*. The first reaction was almost shocked surprise: Everyone present was convinced he knew exactly what was meant by it, and Locke's question was considered almost "frivolous." But then his suggestion was accepted, the physicians proceeded to work out the definition, and soon found that the controversy was due to different interpretations. One party had taken liquor to mean a real liquid (like water or blood) and therefore rejected the idea that such a liquid was flowing through the nerves. The other party interpreted the word as being more in the nature of a "fluid" (a form of energy, like electricity) and was convinced that such a *liquor* did indeed flow through the nerves. After having clarified both interpretations and having accepted the second, the debate was concluded in the shortest possible time with all in favor. [9]

This is an excellent example of the way some people can bring truly scientific discussions to a screeching halt. But even though there will always be some troublemakers like Locke, the witches are very likely to find enough room for ultra-solutions in scientific discussions. A nice example is provided by Molière, showing how the skillful use of definitions can create their own, seemingly objective reality. In one of his comedies a group of eminent doctors is trying to discover why opium causes people to sleep. After a lengthy discussion they conclude that opium produces sleep because it contains a *dormitive principle.*

But back to the "I-know-exactly-what-you-are-thinking" solution. An intriguing suggestion can be found in the book *Fights, Games and Debates* by the Canadian logician Anatol Rapoport [14]. Almost as an aside, he mentions an ingenious idea that has immediate relevance to our present subject. Rather than asking either party in the presence of the opponent for their respective definitions of the problem (thereby putting them at each other's throats in no time), Rapoport suggests inviting party A to present party *B*'s point of view as completely and fully as possible, until B is satisfied with A's description. Then it is B's turn to do the same with *A*'s view of the problem, again until party A finds that *his* point of view has been presented fairly. Rapoport assumed that this technique would probably defuse some of the conflict before the problem itself was discussed. The practical application of this strategy, both in therapy and with organizations larger than a marriage or a family, proves the correctness of Rapoport's assumption. Not infrequently, one of the partners says in amazement and disbelief: "But I had no idea that you thought that I think this . . ." which is already a significant step away from the naïve conviction: "I know exactly what you are thinking."

Quite independently of Rapoport, a similar intervention was developed by the psychiatrist

Mara Selvini-Palazzoli and her collaborators in Milan. She calls it *circular questioning*. It is particularly indicated when a problem-solver wants to arrive as quickly as possible at a reasonably objective understanding of the nature of a relationship between two people. Rather than trying to elicit that information in the way that seems to make most sense, that is, by asking both partners for their respective, individual views, this information is sought from a third person who knows both partners. One of Selvini's examples is taken from a family therapy session in which it became necessary to clarify the relationship between the father and the younger daughter. Rather than trying to get this information from them individually (and then trying to make sense of the contradictions or the silence) the therapist asked the elder daughter to present *her* view of the rapport between father and sister. And Selvini remarks:

. . . Suppose she shows disapproval of certain behaviors of the father in relation to the sister. It would make a big difference in regard to the information concerning the triadic relationship (that is, including the person questioned) if the other two became confused, or if each reacted in the same manner, or if only the father were to protest in indignation while the sister remained cryptically silent or showed a marked hositility or scorn. [18]

It is tempting to fantasize the application of such techniques to international conflicts which—very much like a problematic marriage—are characterized by an abysmal ignorance of the other side's views and intentions, *plus* the unshakable delusion of knowing them exactly. The two superpowers, the United States and the Soviet Union, are a prime example. Their plight is aggravated by the fact that even if a "therapist" could be found to lead them out of their zero-sum game, they would never accept such an intervention. This greatly facilitates Hecate's task, since even the smallest compromise between the superpowers would only delay the nuclear ultra-solution and would thus be most undesirable for her. But the contrary is the case: Lately the witches have been particularly successful in solidifying the stubbornness of the two contestants. This is how they did it:

They convincingly suggested to the Americans that the threat from the East was a purely military one. This made all the more sense since—apart from the Warsaw Pact armies and the Soviet rockets—the East is in no position to threaten the West. And ever since then, Washington has devoted itself, with exemplary fervor, to the research and development of new futuristic weapon systems that sooner or later are likely to blow up.

The Soviet leaders were brainwashed in a much more elegant fashion. They were led to believe that the West threatens them in three ways. First, of course, there is the military threat, which can only be countered by pressing almost the entire economic, industrial and scientific potential of the Eartern bloc into the service of getting and staying ahead of the Western armaments. The regrettable but inevitable consequence of this military concentration is a further tightening of belts on the domestic front and the demand for even greater sacrifices from the Socialist brother nations.

The second threat is of an ideological nature. And this threat is totally one-sided, for the corrupt capitalistic system seems to be immune to ideologies. Those in the West do not even consider it necessary to jam Soviet radio and TV broadcasts, and even the tons of most inspiring propaganda material that can be dumped in the West quite freely does not seem to produce much more than yawns. At the same time, the witches point out, "our people" are not equally immune; somehow the Western ideology of non-ideology is irresistible and fascinating to Soviet citizens. Imagine what might happen if, by way of a military détente, the need for the hermetic encapsulation of the Socialist fatherland became less plausible and such subversive rags as the *London Times* or the *Neue Zürcher Zeitung* could no longer be banned for the same old reasons.

Thirdly, the West represents a grave economic menace. What if, for instance, Western oil companies with their know-how and their technology had to be enlisted to help in the exploration and development of Siberian off-shore oil fields? The entire economic structure of the Eastern bloc would thus be exposed to capitalistic penetration.

The inevitable conclusion of all this: The continued existence of the military threat is less of an evil, by far, than its disappearance. For what would become of the heroic siege mentality and its stabilizing domestic effect, of the obligation of all citizens to protect the fatherland and to keep alive the two-dimensional ideology: "Whosoever is not with me is against me?"

9

Disorder
and Order

W_hy_ should it be so easy to get stuck in the wrong solutions, large or small, and to continue trying more of the same until the ultimate problem-solver, death, applies the final solution? This is a question open to endless speculation. For classical science the answer lies in the Second Law of Thermodynamics, according to which all natural processes have a tendency to proceed from order to disorder, to degrade as a result of the constant loss of energy from very complex structures to a uniform, undifferentiated state. The measure of this disorder is called *entropy*. But the opposite natural law is also known to both scientists and laymen; that there is an evolution from lower to higher forms of organization, observable everywhere in nature, whose measure is called *negentropy* (i.e. the opposite, or the negation, of entropy). And this is where things become interesting for the professional problem-solver and contra-Hecate partisan, for here we can begin to tie up some of the loose strands from preceding chapters, and a distinguishable pattern begins to emerge.

Suppose we return once more to the example of the trench warfare in Flanders. What deserves special attention is the fact that the live-and-let-live principle was not the result of some agreement between the two opponents—and even less so of individual initiative—but that it developed spontaneously. The principle "somehow" emerged out of that chaos and thereby created its own, concrete reality; a reality which was all the more astonishing since the context in which it took place was deliberately "entropic" in that it was meant to produce a maximum of death and destruction. How then do such "negentropic" structures arise?

To date the answers are still very tentative and even contradictory. We have as yet no way of adequately understanding or predicting the processes that lead from disorder to order. Of course, in the good old days the answer was simple: These processes were the design of higher powers. But this explanation smacks a bit of Molière's *dormitive principle* and merely shifts the weight from one foot to the other.

What concerns us here does not emanate from heaven, but from *within* the particular set of circumstances, although the end result is *more* than and *different from* the nature of these individual circumstances. Some of them were already touched upon in Chapter 2, but here we are less interested in the complications brought about by *more of the same* than in the outcome of interactions between different basic properties.

To move away from the abstract, let us look at a few practical examples. When two atoms of hydrogen and one atom of oxygen enter into a particular pattern of relationship, they form a substance, H_2O, whose properties cannot be reduced to those of the individual atoms of which it is comprised. Water is something *different*, something that is not simply the sum of the individual characteristics of hydrogen and oxygen, and any attempt to grasp its essence by reducing it to those separate ingredients would result in nonsense. But we all tend to pursue nonsense of this kind. Take the simple case of a dyadic relationship, this time not between atoms but between two human beings. We have seen how either partner in case of conflict tends to blame the other. Each is convinced that he or she is doing everything to solve the conflict—and yet the conflict persists and may get worse. This *has* to be the other's fault—for where else could the fault lie? There can be no *third* source of trouble between just *two* people. And yet there is. Every relationship (be it between atoms, cells, organs, humans, nations, etc.) is more than and different from the sum of all the ingredients that the entities involved bring into the relationship. The biologists call this an *emergent quality,* the psychologists a *Gestalt.* But to see this while we are standing *inside* the relationship is nearly impossible.

In exactly this sense, the principle of "live and let live" during World War I in Flanders was due neither to the initiative of one or the other opponent, nor to the work of some skillful mediator, but to "something" that emerged from the basic situation. Once our awareness of these emergent qualities has been sharpened, we can appreciate how decisive they are for our lives. But this is also where everything becomes unacceptable to perfectionists and to the Manicheans. For once accepted, there is no denying that these new forms of order can emerge only where there exists a certain measure of disorder. W. Ross Ashby, one of the founders of cybernetics, used to illustrate this principle with the following example: A tightrope walker can maintain his balance only by constant random movements with his balancing pole. (The same holds true for a bicyclist's movements with the handlebar.) If we now wanted to "perfect" the tightrope walker's style and eliminate these disorderly fluctuations, we might be tempted to grab and steady the balancing pole with the immediate result of making him lose balance and fall off the tightrope. Sounds obvious, doesn't it? Yes, but only in the case of tightrope walkers or bicycle riders. In just about any other instance we may be far from comprehending that order without a certain degree of disorder becomes inimical to life, because it smothers the possibility of negentropy. Ultimate order is an ultra-solution, as many a social innovator (or even a management consultant) has found out as he tried to bring about perfect order.

Needless to say, disorder in and of itself is just as destructive, since it is characterized by entropy pure and simple. What is needed is an interaction between the two: Change is synonymous with the emergence of a new quality, and this emergent quality presupposes and in turn creates a degree of disorder. But this may be threatening for many people, for it is much easier to decry the evils of disorder than those of order. And of course, the witches will do what they can to assure that order and disorder remain enemies.

10

Humanity, Divinity, Bestiality

"He who would do good must do so in minute particulars; the general good is the plea of patriots, politicians and knaves," the British satirist Samuel Butler is supposed to have said.

Nature consistently seems to prove Butler right. Everything that develops, grows and flourishes does so "in minute particulars," quietly, in the smallest steps, while all large changes are catastrophic and cataclysmic. But who can get all fired up about small steps? Utopian vistas are needed to inspire the masses. And moreover, they are so clearly ideal that only an idiot or a malicious misanthrope would fail to embrace them.

This leads us again to ultra-solutions. And perhaps the most classic ultra-solution to the problems standing in the way of the general good can be traced back to Plato. For Plato, the philosopher is no longer the (Socratic) *seeker* of truth, but he *possesses* truth. In other words, he is the beholder of the divine order of things that remains incomprehensible to the dim intellect of the masses. Who, therefore, is more competent than he to guide human destiny and put the commonwealth in order? And as Karl Popper [11] shows convincingly, Plato had no doubt that he was in possession of that ultimate truth.

What follows from such a conviction is an inescapable pseudologic which Plato explains in his *Republic* and elsewhere in detail and without any qualms. For instance: The wisdom of the wisest in and of itself is not enough, it must be imparted to the ignorant—if necessary against their will. This authorizes, nay, obligates the philosopher-king to employ whatever is needed, even untruth, in the service of truth. Every individual interpretation of truth must be suppressed, and to this end Plato recommends institutions that foreshadow the Inquisition and the concentration camps. A race of men must be bred that stands unconditionally behind the leader, the philosopher-king. An important part of the wisdom of the wisest is his awareness that the final happiness of mankind may require and indeed justify certain final solutions—an escalation whose three main steps the Austrian poet Grillparzer described with the inimitably terse formula: *Humanity, divinity, bestiality.*

What is particularly appalling is the realization that these inhuman consequences of the pursuit of truth are by no means deviations from the pure doctrine or simply the result of human blunder, but that they are the logical and ineluctable consequence of what seems a reasonable and altruistic idea, namely that for the benefit of mankind the wisest should rule. But the need to find the wisest creates a paradox: Who is to identify this person? Somebody who is wiser than the wisest? But if there be such a person, should he not then be the ruler? Or do we simply take somebody's word that he is the wisest? Or should the choice be made by those of lesser wisdom? But would not their imperfect wisdom make it impossible for them to agree on who is the wisest?

Or consider this: What decent, responsible and concerned human being would not fully and unconditionally embrace the ideal solution of all social problems expressed in the formula: "To each according to his needs; from each according to his abilities"? It sounds ideal, yes? The only trouble is that this ultra-solution presupposes an abundance of material goods (which no economic system has yet achieved), and a power elite in possession of the ultimate wisdom, enabling it to decide (definitively and beyond all appeal) who needs what and who is capable of what. And if the individual, whose needs and capabilities are thus defined, is not quite of the same opinion, this proves that there is something wrong with *him* and not with the wisdom of the wisest.

Against these electrifying and convincing ultra-solutions, the few voices crying in the wilderness hardly stand a chance. One of them is Karl Popper, the proponent of "small steps" which—precisely because they are small—are scorned by the utopian mind of any world improver. How could such a world improver agree with a social order in which those in power are not intent on establishing the terrestrial Paradise, but, like Popper, ask themselves: "How can we organize our political institutions such that even incompetent and dishonest rulers cannot cause much damage?"[12]

But to return to the starting point of this chapter: The great lies dormant in the small; small causes lead to significant developments; therefore we should respect and protect the small. This thesis has no claim to originality; it is an insight that has been around for a very long time. The following oriental story bears charming witness:

The famous mystic Abu Bakr Shibli died in Baghdad in 945. After his death he appeared to one of his friends in a dream. "How has God treated you?" the friend asked.

And Abu Bakr replied: "As I stood before His throne He asked me: 'Do you know why I have forgiven you?'

I said: 'Because of my good deeds.'

He said: 'No.'

I said: 'Because I was sincere in my worship.'

He again said: 'No.'

And I said: 'Because of my pilgrimages and my fasts and my prayers.'

He replied: 'No, not because of all of this have I forgiven you.'

I said: 'Because of my voyages to acquire knowledge and because I left my home to join the holy.'

He said: 'No.'

I said: 'O Lord, these are the deeds that lead to salvation and these I have placed above everything else, and I thought that because of them you would forgive me.'

And he said: 'No, not on account of all these actions have I forgiven you.'

So I said: 'O Lord, why then?'

And God asked me: 'Do you remember how on a cold winter day you were walking through the streets of Baghdad, and you found a kitten that was exhausted from the cold and ran from corner to corner to find shelter from the icy wind, and you had pity on it and picked it up and put it inside your fur and protected it from the bitter cold?'

I said: 'Yes, I remember.'

He said: 'Because you had pity on that cat, Abu Bakr, because of *that* I have pity on you.' "
[17]

11

Gloomy Sunday

It is a pity that the story of Abu Bakr and the cat does not tell us to what extent he included himself in his kindness. For there are people who do not consider themselves worthy of their own love. At first thought, this may seem improbable, for we know that the Bible already concerns itself with the contrary and asks us to love our neighbor (at least) as much as we love ourselves.

But the exact reverse was the case with János Jankó from the Hungarian town of Varumnyiháza. All right, he was not exactly a philanthropist, but still he was one of these rare people with virtually no enemies. He was old enough to have lived through the nightmarish history of his country since the 1930's. In 1956 he managed to slip away from Hungary and to establish a reasonably satisfactory existence in another country to which his fate had led him, an existence that could be defined as comfortable solitude. All this changed abruptly as he awoke on the morning of his fifty-fifth birthday. There was—probably a carry-over from a dream—the faint hum of the melancholy gypsy tune "Gloomy Sunday" in his ear, and for hours he could not get rid of it. My readers may not know that this tune has a notorious history: During the years of János Jankó's adolescence the tune triggered a veritable wave of suicide in his home country—which has always had a penchant for this kind of ultra-solution—so much so that playing the song in public had eventually been prohibited by law. Needless to say, this "solution" had made "Gloomy Sunday" even more famous, and thus known to many more people.

In Jankó's case, it would be difficult to say whether it was the effect of the remembered tune or the fact that it was his birthday (and a Sunday, to boot) that caused him to take stock of his life. And the result was that he did not like himself anymore. It was as if his inner peace now turned out to have been merely an armistice, and a smoldering conflict that had always been there, had now burst into the open. Had it been possible to look into Jankó *from outside*, one might have seen a murderous situation between *two* people: Between a cruel, medieval potentate and his helpless captive, whom he threatened constantly, starved and deprived of his sleep. Of course, János Jankó himself did not see his situation that way. He was aware only of a feeling of emptiness and of growing hatred towards himself which he had never experienced so intensely towards anybody else. That he also felt himself vaguely threatened, that he lost weight and could not sleep, were side effects that could not be explained. His doctor was unable to discover any physical causes.

The months passed, but not the coldness and emptiness of Jankó's world. His modest material needs were adequately met, he was healthy and reasonably satisfied with the everyday aspects of his life, but this only increased his feeling that he had no right and no reason to be so depressed. So what was the point of it all? If life made no sense, what sense was there in living?

And one day, unexpectedly, as with "Gloomy Sunday", Dostoevsky's *Demons* came to his mind, especially that scene where Kirillov explains that Christ's death proves the senselessness of the world. Jankó looked it up and read:

Listen: that Man was the loftiest of all on earth,
He was that who gave meaning to life. The whole

planet, with everything on it, is mere madness without him. There has never been any like Him before or since, never, up to a miracle. For that is the miracle, that there never was and never will be another like Him. And if that is so, if the laws of nature did not even spare Him, have not even spared their miracle and made Him live in a lie and die for a lie, then all the planet is a lie and rests on a lie and mockery. So then, the very laws of the planet are a lie and a vaudeville of devils. What is there to live for? Answer, if you are a man.

A physicist might have said that Kirillov had understood the entropy of all existence. And this would have been equally true for János Jankó. In any case, he now was ready: The solution was death and, as with Kirillov, his pistol was the means of achieving it. Or, at least, that is how *he* saw it. Again, seen from outside, one might have concluded that the potentate had decided to execute his victim. Be that as it may, what mattered was that Jankó had now arrived at a firm decision, a decision that transformed a prevailing mood into an imminent fact. And at this point Jankó suddenly realized that twice before he had been near that threshold.

First, there was that experience several years earlier which to him had seemed like a strange lesson from an unknown power. Like many of us, Janko had firmly and proudly resolved that in the event of an incurable illness he would initially accept it, submit—out of respect for his own life—to whatever medical treatment appeared reasonable, but reserve the right to put an end to his suffering when it became unbearable. It so happened that one day his physician discovered a swelling, could not in good conscience rule out a tumor, and insisted on a tissue examination. For forty-eight hours Jankó had to wait for the pathologist's report. And suddenly his cool determination was gone. Suddenly death was no longer a solution. Only life mattered, not perhaps out of immature cowardice, and this surprised him more than anything else. The mere *possibility* of imminent death created in him respect for life. And this did not change even when he was told that the lump was benign and there was no reason to worry.

The other experience belonged to his more distant past, to those years when Jankó and countless others not only found themselves deprived of the most basic essentials, but survival was threatened in a diabolically three-fold way: First by the occupants of his country and the final solution practiced by them; secondly by their constantly advancing enemies; and thirdly by the nightly bomb carpets laid by those who alone could be expected to re-establish a sane and free world. At that time as well, he had had a pistol, but not until now had he realized that not once in all those months of hunger and terror had he thought about the senselessness of the world, but only about survival. It was what George Orwell must have meant when he wrote in one of his essays: People with empty bellies never despair of the universe, or even think about it, for that matter.

Only after these reminiscences did it become obvious to Jankó that in spite of his despair and disgust, turning himself into a corpse was not the solution. What he wanted, what he desperately sought, was something totally different, a fundamental change. And so he rejected the ultra-solution of the pistol, and at this same moment re-entered the service of negentropy. To put it less "scientifically," he stepped outside the Manichean opposites, "emptiness of life" or "emptiness of death," and began the labyrinthine quest for meaning.

12

Is It *This*?

Mirages must be approached before they reveal themselves as mirages. Wrong paths must be taken in order to discover that they lead nowhere. This truism is in accordance with the so-called *constructivist* view—the study of the processes by which we create our own realities. It postulates that all we can ever hope to know of the "real" reality (if it exists at all) is what it is *not*. One of the main exponents of radical constructivism, the psychologist Ernst von Glasersfeld, puts it as follows:

. . .Knowledge can be seen as something that the organism builds up in the attempt to order the as such amorphous flow of experience by establishing repeatable experiences and relatively reliable relations between them. The possibilities of constructing such an order are determined and perpetually constrained by the preceding steps in the construction. This means that the "real" world manifests itself exclusively there where our constructions break down. But since we can describe and explain these breakdowns only in the very concepts that we have used to build the failing structures, this process can never yield a picture of the world which we could hold responsible for their failure. [6]

This perspective has the advantage that it introduces a common denominator into that *smörgåsbord* of solutions, pseudo-solutions and ultra-solutions of which this book is composed—or so at least I hope. And in a perhaps somewhat megalomaniacal vein I wish to bolster my argument by invoking Wittgenstein's remark in the *Tractatus* (proposition 6.45), where he, too, speaks of that certain need to go wrong:

My propositions are elucidatory in this way: he who understands me finally recognizes them as senseless, when he has climbed out through them, on them, over them. (He must so to speak throw away the ladder, after he has climbed up on it.)

Is It This?

At this point, after all these propositions, the time has come to return to "our man" whom we left at the end of the first chapter. For simplicity's sake let us now assume that it was *he* who in his search for security, certainty, and final happiness had taken all the wrong paths described here—and not only these. In a very real sense, he had turned into a modern romanticist, into the reincarnation of those eighteenth-century seekers, consumed by their longing for what one of them, the poet Novalis, had symbolized as the Blue Flower—that miraculous flower that blossoms somewhere in the unknown and whose finding was the ultimate fulfillment of the romantics' nostalgia. He had read Novalis at school and had been deeply touched by his work, but only now did it dawn on him that he was himself one of those seekers. Until then this most basic motif of his life had remained unknown to him, precisely because he was so totally involved with it. This insight was followed soon by a second one which stemmed from the first, but at the same time seemed to cast doubt on it: The romanticists seemed to *know* what they were seeking; but our man was seeking without knowing what. Not only did he not know *where* to find it, but even what *it* was. Yet, in spite of this, he now understood that at every moment of his life, even during his most insignificant actions, he was incessantly asking: Is it *this?*

What other way was there to search for
something for which one thirsts "as the hart
panteth after the water brooks"—and yet one
does not even know its *name?* Unfortunately
our man had not read the *Tao Te Ching,* for
there he would have found a partial answer to
the problem of naming:

> The Tao that can be expressed
> is not the real Tao;
> the name that can be named
> is not the real name.

Or, like Faust, our man could have said of
himself:

> Through all the world I only raced:
> Whatever I might crave, I laid my hands on,
> what would not do, I would abandon,
> and what escaped, I would let go.
> I only would desire and attain,
> and wish for more . . .

Thus, whatever he "laid his hands on" and
asked "Is it *this?*" the answer produced was
never more than "This is not it."

Again and again he found himself empty-
handed, but invariably he drew what seemed
the only possible conclusion from these disap-
pointments, namely that the particular *this*
was not *it,* that he had not yet given *it* the right
name, had not searched for it in the right place.

Sometimes that unknown fulfillment was attached to a certain goal whose attainment took years, inspired him to exceptional achievements, and earned him great admiration, but upon reaching the goal, it did not hold what it had seemed to promise. The disappointment felt by our man was put so well by Shakespeare:

> ... Mad in pursuit, and in possession so
> Had, in having, and in quest to have, extreme,
> A bliss in prove, and proved a very woe,
> Before, a joy proposed, behind, a dream.

Any such mirage fades when we approach it and immediately regains its irresistible attractiveness as soon as we turn away or lose it. How often our man attached his longing to distant places and was convinced (*how* he arrived at these convictions he was unable to explain to himself) that reaching these places would give him a totally different sense of self, of harmony with the world, only to find these experiences withheld when he arrived there! Discouragement and emptiness awaited and accompanied him as he wandered through these cities and valleys. He felt the same as he had always felt before; unfulfilled and unchanged. But then, almost immediately after his departure from a place, disappointed, the longing for the same place returned in its old intensity—as if he had not already discovered that *this* was not *it*. And so he travelled there again, back into the same disillusionment. Just as often it was a woman who, before she surrendered to him, was the embodiment of all his longing—and then only another body. Soon the bitter separation came and with it the return of the illusion, only now rendered even more intense by the feeling of paradise lost. And again emptiness.

He felt abandoned, cheated, rejected. Had he believed in God he would have accused Him of not letting him come home. But since he was an atheist, he occasionally toyed with the ultrasolution of suicide, for his despair grew until it seemed to envelop him. Why continue to live?

And yet, seen from *outside,* our man's plight was rather banal. He only questioned the *fruits* of his quest, not the quest *itself.* This made the quest endless, for the number of potential discoveries is infinite. What even the Romantics had not taken into account was the trivial possibility that the Blue Flower did not exist *at all*—and not that the seeker had not yet sought for it in the right place. Seen from this perspective, there seems no solution except for the Manichean opposites of finding or not finding, and this was the zero-sum game with himself in which our man was caught.

It is very difficult to show clearly and convincingly how he eventually became aware of the possibility of escape. One contributing element was the undeniable fact that fate rarely denied him the arrival at whatever goal seemed to him to be *the* goal. For, as we have seen, there is nothing more sobering than a fulfilled hope, and nothing more seductive than an unfulfilled one.

He had reached the point at which he was fully aware of his quest and with it of his perennial question: Is it *this?* And then, one day, a minute change occurred, one of those which are small enough to effect great results. As improbable as it may seem, it was nothing but the tiny shift in emphasis from *this* to *it*— whereupon the question suddenly became: "Is *it* this?" Immediately the answer presented itself to him: No *this* out there, no thing in the world can ever be more than a *name* of *it*—and names are nothing but empty sounds. At this moment, the separation between him and *it* fell away; or, as the philosophers would define it, the separation between subject and object. No *this* could ever be *it. What the world does not hold, it cannot withhold,* he kept saying aloud to himself, and also the strangely significant words: *I am more myself than I.* Now it was clear that the only reason for not having found what he had searched for all his life was the search *itself;* he now realized that we cannot find out there in the world and thus can never *have* what we already *are.*

And with this, the words of the Apocalypse that "time shall be no more" fulfilled itself for him—and he fell into the eternity of the present moment.

But only for a second did he remain in this

timelessness, for in order to hold on to it and *have* it forever, he immediately resorted to the ultra-solution of giving the experience a name and of seeking its repetition. . . .

Bibliography

1. Ashworth, Tony. *Trench Warfare 1914–1918; The Live and Let Live System.* Holmes & Meier Publishers, New York, 1980.
2. Berdyaev, Nicholas. *Dostoevsky.* Meridian Books, New York, 1957.
3. Fogelman, Eva, and Valerie L. Wiener. "The Few, the Brave, the Noble." *Psychology Today* August 1985.
4. Gall, John. *Systemantics.* Pocket Books, New York, 1978.
5. Gheorghiu, C. Virgil. *The Twenty-Fifth Hour* (translated by Rita Eldon). Henry Regnery Company, Chicago, 1950.
6. Glasersfeld, Ernst von. "An Introduction to Radical Constructivism." In *The Invented Reality,* Paul Watzlawick (ed.). W. W. Norton, New York, 1984.

7. Jung, Carl G. *Symbols of Transformation*. Bollingen Foundation, New York 1952.
8. Kreuzer, Franz (ed.). *Neue Welt aus Null und Eins (World of Zero and One)*. Franz Deuticke, Vienna, 1985.
9. Leisi, Ernst. "Falsche Daten hochpräzis verarbeitet." *Neue Zürcher Zeitung*, No. 301, 28/29 December 1985.
10. Lübbe, Hermann. "Ideologische Selbstermächtigung zur Gewalt." *Neue Zürcher Zeitung*, No. 251, 28/29 October 1978.
11. Popper, Karl R. *The Open Society and its Enemies*. Harper, New York, 1963.
12. Popper, Karl R. "Woran glaubt der Westen?" In *Auf der Suche nach einer besseren Welt*, by Karl R. Popper. Piper, Munich, 1984.
13. Postman, Neil. *Amusing Ourselves to Death*. Viking, New York, 1984.
14. Rapoport, Anatol. *Fights, Games and Debates*. University of Michigan, Ann Arbor, 1960.
15. Revel, Jean-François. *How Democracies Perish*. Doubleday, Garden City 1983.
16. Revel, Jean-François. "Die Demokratien im Angesicht der Totalitarismen." Summary, Piper Information, Munich, 1984.
17. Schimmel, Annemarie (ed.) *Die orientalische Katze* (adapted from the German translation). Eugen Diederichs, Cologne, 1983.
18. Selvini-Palazzoli, Mara, et al.: "Hypothesizing—Circularity—Neutrality: Three Guidelines for the Conductor of Sessions." *Family Process* 19:3–12, 1980.
19. Watzlawick, Paul. *The Language of Change*. Basic Books, New York, 1978.

Printed in the United States
96280LV00001B/20/A

32880971R00068

Made in the USA
Middletown, DE
08 January 2019